SPORTS ZONE

HOCKEY
A Guide for Players and Fans

BY HEATHER WILLIAMS

CAPSTONE PRESS
a capstone imprint

Fact Finders Books are published by Capstone
1710 Roe Crest Drive, North Mankato, Minnesota 56003
www.capstonepub.com

Editorial Credits
Lauren Dupuis-Perez, editor; Sara Radka, designer;
Eric Gohl, media researcher; Laura Manthe, production specialist

Photo Credits
Flickr: City of Vancouver Archives/Stuart Thomson, 6; Getty Images: Al Bello, cover (foreground), 22, Allsport/Glenn Cratty, 29, Bruce Bennett, 4, Christian Petersen, 17, Dennis Pajot, 23, Allsport/Scott Halleran, 28 (bottom), Jared Wickerham, 24, Mike Ehrmann, 20, Rob Carr, 19, Steve Powell, 25, Trevor Lush, cover (background); Pixabay: intographics, background; Shutterstock: Andrey_Popov, 12 (top), Lucky Business, 27, Matthew Jacques, 14, Nicholas Piccillo, 18, Ronnie Chua, 28 (top), SebStock, 8–9, Steve Gilbert, 10–11, stockphoto-graf, 12 (bottom); Wikimedia: Library and Archives Canada/William James Topley, 9, Unknown, 7

Library of Congress Cataloging-in-Publication Data
Names: Williams, Heather author.
Title: Hockey : a guide for players and fans / by Heather Williams.
Description: First Edition. | North Mankato, Minnesota : An imprint of Capstone Press, [2019] | Series: Fact Finders. Sports Zone
Identifiers: LCCN 2019005982| ISBN 9781543573596 (Hardcover) | ISBN 9781543574586 (Paperback) | ISBN 9781543573718 (eBook PDF)
Subjects: LCSH: Hockey—Juvenile literature.
Classification: LCC GV847.25 .W554 2019 | DDC 796.962—dc23
LC record available at https://lccn.loc.gov/2019005982

TABLE OF CONTENTS

Introduction 4

From Field to Ice 6

Gearing Up 10

Rules of the Rink 14

Defend and Attack 20

Getting Started 26

Glossary 30

Read More 31

Internet Sites 31

Index 32

Team captain Meghan Duggan and her teammate Hilary Knight both have three Olympic medals. They earned silver at the 2010 and 2014 games, and gold in 2018.

Snow falls outside the Gangneung Hockey Centre in Pyeongchang, South Korea. The 2018 Winter Olympics are coming to a close. Inside, almost 5,000 people are watching the women's ice hockey gold medal game. The United States and Canada have battled for 80 minutes. The score is 2–2 after overtime. The two teams prepare for a **shoot-out**.

After five shots per team, the game remains tied. A second shoot-out begins. American player Jocelyne Lamoureux-Davidson makes the score 3–2. When Canadian Meghan Agosta takes the next shot, U.S. goaltender Maddie Rooney is ready. Rooney blocks Agosta's shot. The United States wins the gold medal! It is the first time the U.S. women's team has won hockey gold since 1998.

Hockey was born in Canada more than 200 years ago. But while the action-packed sport has roots in Canada, the U.S. women's team is proof that ice hockey can be anyone's game.

shoot-out—a method of breaking a tie score at the end of overtime play

People have been playing ball and stick games for hundreds of years. Before ice hockey, there were games like hurley and shinty. They are games played on a field with sticks and a small ball. Native Americans invented lacrosse, and they played a game like it on ice and snow. In around 1800, students in Nova Scotia, Canada, started playing hurley on their local ice skating ponds during the winter months. Ice hockey was born.

Early hockey uniforms were more for protection from the cold than protection from injury.

A Canadian named James Creighton grew up playing an early form of ice hockey in Nova Scotia. In the late 1800s, he moved to Montreal, Canada. Creighton introduced his new friends to ice hockey. He even made up the some of the game's very first rules. People all over Montreal started playing ice hockey. They even played on indoor ice rinks. The first official public game of indoor hockey was played in Montreal in 1875.

James Creighton was a part of almost every hockey game played in Montreal during the sport's first years.

Creighton was a student at McGill University. He started the first college hockey team there in 1877. He taught everyone his rules. He also replaced the ball with a flat disc. More people started playing ice hockey. Teams began to form all over Canada. The first hockey club was founded in Montreal. Ice hockey had become Canada's favorite sport.

The National Hockey League (NHL) was started in 1917. There were four teams in the NHL when it began. All of them were from Canada. The Boston Bruins became the first American team in the NHL in 1924. In 1926 the NHL began giving a trophy called the Stanley Cup to the best NHL team. Today the NHL is made up of 31 teams. There are 24 teams from the United States and seven from Canada.

Ice hockey became an Olympic sport in the 1920s. Canada won gold six times in the first seven Olympic games with ice hockey. Other countries, such as Russia and the United States, then started winning medals too. Ice hockey is still Canada's national sport, but the country has many tough rivals to play.

1875 · · · · · · ·

1892 · · · · · ·

1909 · · · · · ·

1924 · · · · · · ·

2008 · · · · · ·

amateur—describes a sports league that athletes take part in for pleasure rather than for money

James Creighton organizes the first public indoor hockey match at Victoria Skating Rink in Montreal, Canada.

The first Stanley Cup is awarded to a team from the Montreal **Amateur** Athletic Association.

The Stanley Cup

In 1892 the leader of Canada, Lord Frederick Stanley, decided ice hockey needed an official trophy. It stands almost 3 feet (1 meter) high. The names of all the players on the winning team are carved on the cup every year. A new ring is added to the cup when there is no more space for names. Each winning player gets to keep the cup for one day. Three babies have been baptized in the Stanley Cup. It has even been used as an ice cream bowl and a flower pot!

The Montreal Canadiens form. The team is the oldest professional ice hockey team in the world.

The Boston Bruins become the first U.S. team in the National Hockey League, which was formed in 1917.

The Detroit Red Wings win the Stanley Cup for the 11th time in the sport's history, the most of any U.S. team.

The first ice hockey games were played with a curved stick and a small ball. The puck was introduced around 1860. Some of the first pucks were slices of large tree branches. The first hockey skates were iron blades fastened to the bottoms of players' shoes or boots. They were attached to shoes with leather straps. Helmets, elbow pads, and other safety gear were invented in the 1920s and 1930s. But most players did not wear them in those days.

4

5

3

1. Stick

The first hockey sticks were carved from a single piece of wood. Today most are made of graphite, fiberglass, or a mix of all three.

2. Puck

Today's hockey pucks are made of hard rubber. They are frozen before games to make them less bouncy.

3. Skates

The best hockey skates provide good ankle support for players. The blades must be sharpened often so players can control their movement on the ice.

4. Helmet

All ice hockey players are required to wear a helmet with a face shield or mask. Many helmets have an attached mouth guard.

5. Shoulder Pads

Players are required to wear shoulder, elbow, knee, and shin protectors.

graphite—a strong, lightweight material made from a gray or black mineral

fiberglass—a strong, lightweight material made from woven threads of glass

Gear for the Game

Before safety gear was required, ice hockey players had many injuries. Ice hockey is a fast-paced game. Players can get hit by sticks, flying pucks, and other players. Sprains and bruises are common in ice hockey. Players can also have head and mouth injuries. Without safety gear, ice hockey would be very dangerous! Helmets, masks, pads, guards, and gloves help players stay safe during the action.

Hockey gloves have short cuffs to allow for better stick handling.

FACT

Some of the first hockey pucks were made from cut up rubber balls, slices of tree branches, and even frozen cow droppings.

Most helmets have attached masks. Helmets and face masks protect the eyes, teeth, and skull. Players also strap on pads to protect shoulders, hips, chest, and elbows. Padded hockey pants protect the thighs, tailbone, and hips, and close-fitting guards attach to the legs, knees, and shins. These items allow movement while shielding players' bones. Players also wear padded gloves to cover the wrists and finger joints.

Ice hockey goaltenders wear all of this safety gear, plus extra goaltender gear. Goaltenders, also known as goalies, must deal with high-speed pucks. They often dive onto the ice to block shots. They sometimes crash into opposing players. The goaltender's gear is like a suit of armor. The leg pads for goaltenders are wide and thick with padding. They give the goalie extra protection and help them block pucks. Goaltenders also wear special gloves called blockers to stop pucks. A goalie in the NHL wears up to 50 pounds (23 kilograms) of safety gear!

sprain—a violent straining or wrenching of the parts around a joint, without dislocation

RULES OF THE RINK

There are a few basic rules for all ages and levels of ice hockey. There are rules for what equipment players need. There are rules about what each player can do during a game. There are also rules about the ice. Every ice hockey rink has what is called a **face-off** circle in the center. The rink also has a red middle line, two blue lines, and two goal lines. The area behind the blue line is the defending zone. The area behind the other team's blue line is the offensive zone. The space between the two blue lines is the neutral zone. It does not belong to either team.

When a player passes the puck across all of the zones on the rink it is called icing. If a player is not behind the puck when it crosses the other team's blue line, it is called offsides. If icing or offsides are called, play is stopped and restarted with a face-off.

face-off—when a player from each team battles for possession of the puck to start or restart play

There are six players per team on the ice at one time. This is true for every age and level of ice hockey. One player is the goaltender. The goalie works hard to keep the puck from going into the goal. There are two defensemen on a team, one right and one left. They try to keep the puck from making it to the goalie. The left wing, right wing, and center forwards are in charge of scoring. They are good passers. They can control the puck around the goal. These players must get past the other team's defensemen and goalie.

Ice hockey games have three periods. Each period can be as long as 20 minutes, as in the NHL. Periods in youth games can be as short as 12 minutes each. Coaches can make as many substitutions as they want during a game. The game does not stop for subs.

substitution—in sports, when one player is used in place of another player; also called a sub

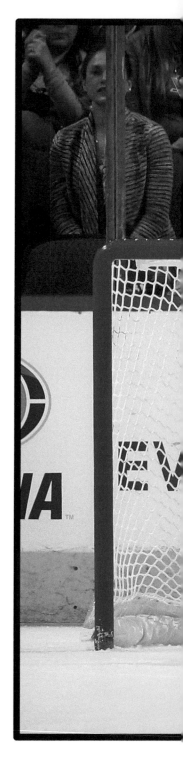

If the offense is putting a lot of pressure on the goalie, he or she may hold or trap the puck. But if the goalie holds the puck without offensive pressure around the goal, it might be considered a rule violation.

Every ice hockey game has officials, people who make sure players stick to the rules. Officials use hand signals to let players know when a rule has been broken. They have to watch every minute of the game carefully. Some parts of ice hockey, such as body checking, can lead to penalties. Checking is when a player uses a part of his or her body to disrupt an opponent and try to get the puck. Checking is allowed once players are 13, but only for boys. In girls' and women's ice hockey, checking is not allowed. Illegal checking leads to a penalty.

An NHL team can earn between 200 and 400 penalties in a single season.

penalty—a punishment for breaking the rules

There are three types of penalties, minor, major, and misconduct.

A penalty in ice hockey is like a timeout for a player. He or she has to leave the game without a sub. Some small penalties include tripping, holding, and hooking another player with the stick. These are two-minute penalties. Big penalties, such as fighting, can lead to a five-minute penalty or even being taken out of the rest of the game. When a player is serving a penalty, his or her team plays with only four players. This is called a penalty kill. The other team still has five players on the ice, which gives them an advantage called a power play.

FACT

In the NHL, if both of a team's goalies are injured the team can appoint any available goalkeeper. This includes a person who might be sitting in the crowd.

DEFEND AND ATTACK

Vladimir Tarasenko has scored more than 30 points for the St. Louis Blues every season since 2014.

All hockey players have to start with the **fundamentals**. The most important ice hockey fundamental is skating. Players must be able to skate fast, both forward and backward. They also have to be able to stop quickly, make sharp turns, and change directions. Players should be able to skate with the puck close in front of them. They should also be good at passing the puck to other players.

Shooting is also a basic ice hockey skill. There are four main types of shots. A slap shot is when a player raises his or her stick up high and swings the stick down. Slap shots often are hard and straight. A wrist shot is when a player turns the stick quickly with his or her wrists. This causes the puck to spin up and off the ice. A backhand shot means that a player strikes the puck with the outer part of the stick.

fundamental—a basic idea or necessary part

Defense

Defense is what a team does to keep the other team from scoring. The key to a winning ice hockey team is a strong defense. A strong defense has a goaltender who moves quickly and is not afraid to dive after the puck. The defensemen on the ice are important too. They try to keep shots from reaching the goaltender. Defensemen can block shots with their bodies or sticks.

P.K. Subban of the Nashville Predators is one of the top defensemen in the NHL. He is also a strong scorer, with an average of 10 goals per season.

In a 2015 Ontario Hockey League game, forward Adam Timleck of the Peterborough Petes checked defenseman Mikhail Sergachev of the Windsor Spitfires against the dasher boards.

One way defensemen help win games is by pressuring the other team's offense. This can mean blocking an opponent's path and not letting him or her pass or shoot. When defensemen pressure the other team's offense, they give their left and right wing and center teammates a chance to take the puck from the other team and try to score. Defensemen can also steal the puck from an opponent and clear it. This means they pass it to a teammate who is in the neutral zone.

From 2011 to 2019, right wing Wayne Simmonds scored 203 goals for the Philadelphia Flyers.

Offense

Offense in ice hockey is all about scoring goals. The center and wingers often work together to move the puck into the offensive zone. They have to get past the other team's defense to get a clear shot on goal. A team sometimes tries to be faster than their opponent's defense. This leaves the goalie with no help and makes scoring easier.

Fakes are a strategy many players use to get past a tough defense. Faking a move means a player will pretend to go one way. He or she then will quickly go the other way. Faking a pass is when a player moves his or her stick to make a pass. He or she then switches direction or moves down the ice with the puck instead of passing. Quick passing is another important offensive skill. Teams that are good at keeping the puck moving wear down the other team's defense.

The "Miracle on Ice"

In the 1980s, the Soviet Union was one of the strongest countries in the world. It also had the world's best ice hockey team. From 1956 to 1976, they won five gold medals at the Olympics. At the 1980 Olympics, the U.S. ice hockey team made it to the final round of the tournament. They had to play the Soviets. The players on the U.S. team were very young. No one expected them to win. They did win, and some people called it a miracle. A group of college boys had taken down a giant. Two days later, the United States beat Finland and won the gold medal.

Not everyone can play ice hockey in the Olympics, but anyone can learn to play. Ice hockey is a great sport for boys and girls of all ages. The best place to start is at an ice rink. Kids can start with a program called Learn to Skate USA. Kids who can skate can take a class called Learn to Play. These classes take place at ice rinks across the United States. Kids should also watch hockey on TV or in person if there is a local team. Watching games is a great way to understand the rules.

Practicing the basics off the ice is another great way to start. Many kids learn ice hockey by playing street hockey. Street hockey is played on a street or parking lot with roller skates, hockey sticks, and a ball. Running and stretching often, eating a healthy diet, and drinking lots of water are also important.

Ice hockey helps kids build their coordination, balance, teamwork, and communication skills.

Joining a Team

A new player can find a team at a local ice rink. Many cities have indoor ice rinks with hockey teams for all ages. Some teams are coed. Some teams are boys-only or girls-only. Girls and boys often play together until they are in middle school.

Players cannot join a team without the right equipment. It is very important for gear to fit well. Going to a sporting goods store to try on equipment is better than buying it online. Some sporting goods stores have great deals on used equipment since young players outgrow their gear faster.

FACT

Manon Rhéaume is the first and only woman to play in the NHL. The Canadian goaltender played in preseason games with the Tampa Bay Lightning in 1992 and 1993.

Wayne Gretzky

Wayne Gretzky is one of the greatest ice hockey players of all time. When he was 6 years old, he played on a team with 10-year-olds. He became a professional player when he was 17. Gretzky helped the Edmonton Oilers win four Stanley Cups. He also played for the Los Angeles Kings, the St. Louis Blues, and the New York Rangers. He scored 894 goals in his career. No other player has scored that many. He is known as "The Great One."

The most important tip for a beginning ice hockey player is to stick with it. Players only get better by playing and practicing. It might be hard at first, but it will be worth the hard work!

coed—including both boys and girls

Glossary

amateur *(AM-uh-chur)*—describes a sports league that athletes take part in for pleasure rather than for money

coed *(KOH-ed)*—including both boys and girls

face-off *(FAYSS-awf)*—when a player from each team battles for possession of the puck to start or restart play

fiberglass *(FY-buhr-glas)*—a strong, lightweight material made from woven threads of glass

fundamental *(FUHN-duh-men-tuhl)*—a basic idea or necessary part

graphite *(GRA-fite)*—a strong, lightweight material made from a gray or black mineral

penalty *(PEN-uhl-tee)*—a punishment for breaking the rules

shoot-out *(SHOOT-out)*—a method of breaking a tie score at the end of overtime play

sprain *(SPRAYN)*—a violent straining or wrenching of the parts around a joint, without dislocation

substitution *(SUHB-stuh-too-shun)*—in sports, when one player is used in place of another player; also called a sub

Read More

Chandler, Matt. *The Science of Hockey: The Top 10 Ways Science Affects the Game.* Top 10 Science. North Mankato, MN: Capstone Press, 2016.

Frederick, Shane. *Hockey Stats and the Stories Behind Them: What Every Fan Needs to Know.* Sports Stats and Stories. North Mankato, MN: Capstone Press, 2016.

Nagelhout, Ryan. *20 Fun Facts About Hockey.* Fun Fact File: Sports! New York: Gareth Stevens Publishing, 2016.

Nagle, Jeanne. *Sidney Crosby: One of the NHL's Top Scorers.* Living Legends of Sports. New York: Britannica Educational Publishing, 2016.

Internet Sites

Ice Hockey
www.dkfindout.com/us/sports/ice-hockey

Pro Hockey Hall of Fame
www.hhof.com

Sports Illustrated Kids Hockey
www.sikids.com/hockey

Index

Canada (Canadian), 5, 6, 7, 8, 9, 28

Creighton, James, 7, 9

defense, 16, 22, 23, 24, 25

equipment, 10, 11, 12, 13, 15, 28

Gretzky, Wayne, 29

Learn to Skate USA, 26

"Miracle on Ice," The, 25

National Hockey League (NHL), 8, 13, 16, 19, 28

offense, 15, 23, 24, 25

Olympics, 5, 8, 25, 26

penalties, 18, 19

Rhéaume, Manon, 28

rules, 7, 14, 15, 18, 26

scoring, 16, 22, 23, 24, 25, 29

Stanley Cup, 8, 9, 29

street hockey, 26